W9-CPF-349

Text
STYLES

HOW TO WRITE AN ADVENTURE STORY

Natalie Hyde

🌳 Crabtree Publishing Company

www.crabtreebooks.com

Text STYLES

Author: Natalie Hyde

**Publishing plan research
  and series development:** Reagan Miller

Editor: Anastasia Suen

Proofreader: Wendy Scavuzzo

Logo design: Samantha Crabtree

Print coordinator: Katherine Berti

Production coordinator and prepress technician:
  Margaret Amy Salter

Photographs:
Library of Congress: page 12 (Alice in Wonderland cover)
Shutterstock: aGinger: page 26 (bottom left
Wikimedia Commons: Trialsanderrors: page 4 (Kidnapped
  cover); Scyld Norning: page 4 (Swiss Family
  Robinson cover); Beeswaxcandle: pages 6, 23 (bottom);
  Theornamentalist: page 12 (The Jungle Book cover);
  Angelprincess72: page 16 (top right); Spangineer:
  pages 16 (bottom left), 22 (top left), 23 (top); Library
  of Congress: page 22 (bottom left); IndianCaverns:
  page 22 (middle right)
All other images by Shutterstock

Library and Archives Canada Cataloguing in Publication

Hyde, Natalie, 1963-, author
       How to write an adventure story / Natalie Hyde.

(Text styles)
Includes index.
Issued in print and electronic formats.
ISBN 978-0-7787-1655-6 (bound).--ISBN 978-0-7787-1660-0 (pbk.).--
ISBN 978-1-4271-9865-5 (pdf).--ISBN 978-1-4271-9870-9 (html)

       1. Adventure stories--Authorship--Juvenile literature. I. Title.
II. Series: Text styles

PN3377.5.A37H93 2014   j808.3'87   C2014-903774-0
                                                    C2014-903775-9

Library of Congress Cataloging-in-Publication Data

Hyde, Natalie, 1963- author.
 How to write an adventure story / Natalie Hyde.
    pages cm. -- (Text styles)
 Includes index.
 ISBN 978-0-7787-1655-6 (reinforced library binding) -- ISBN 978-0-
7787-1660-0 (pbk.) -- ISBN 978-1-4271-9865-5 (electronic pdf) --
ISBN 978-1-4271-9870-9 (electronic html)
 1. Adventure stories--Authorship--Juvenile literature. I. Title.

 PN3377.5.A37H93 2014
 808.3'87--dc23

                                                    2014022776

Crabtree Publishing Company

www.crabtreebooks.com   1-800-387-7650

Printed in Hong Kong/082014/BK2014061?

**Published in Canada
Crabtree Publishing**
616 Welland Ave.
St. Catharines, Ontario
L2M 5V6

**Published in the United States
Crabtree Publishing**
PMB 59051
350 Fifth Avenue, 59th Floor
New York, New York 10118

**Published in the United Kingdom
Crabtree Publishing**
Maritime House
Basin Road North, Hove
BN41 1WR

**Published in Australi
Crabtree Publishing**
3 Charles Street
Coburg North
VIC 3058

CONTENTS

What Is an Adventure Story?	4
Prose, Poem, or Drama?	5
The Voyages of Dr. Doolittle	6
Characters in Adventure Stories	9
Dialogue: Formal and Informal Speech	11
Setting: Where Are We?	12
Plot: A Story In Three Acts	13
Theme: What Is It About?	14
Creative Response to the Adventure Story	15
Black Beauty	16
Setting: Using Your Senses	20
Point of View: Who Is Talking?	22
Plot: A Map of the Story	24
Theme: What Is It About?	25
Creative Response to the Adventure Story	26
Writing an Adventure Story	27
Glossary	31
Index and Further Resources	32

What could be more exciting than finding a lost treasure? Or exploring a hidden city? Or surviving dangers to find your way home? These exciting events can be found in adventure stories. An **adventure story** describes a tale that has risk and danger. Adventure stories are full of action. Some are based on real events in history. Adventure stories are fun to read. They are an escape from the everyday world. In this book, you will learn about the characteristics of adventure stories. You will read adventure stories and learn how to write one of your own!

Kidnapped by Robert Louis Stevenson is set in Scotland. One of the characters is Alan Breck Stewart. He was a freedom fighter who really lived.

THE FIRST ADVENTURE STORIES

The type of adventure stories we know were first written in the 1800s. In those days, many parts of the world were still unknown. These early stories were tales of finding lost cities or being stranded on an island.

Swiss Family Robinson is the story of a family of six. They are shipwrecked on an island in the Pacific. They have to find a way to survive.

PROSE, POEM, OR DRAMA?

Stories can be written down in different ways. In literature, we use different names to talk about the way words are used. The example below shows the same part of a story called *The Voyages of Dr. Doolittle* written in three different ways: as **prose**, a **poem**, and a **drama**.

DRAMA

TIME: Early morning in the springtime

PLACE: On a cobblestone road in a little town called Puddleby-on-the-Marsh

[MATTHEW MUGG, the CAT'S-MEAT MAN, is pulling his cart and talking to TOMMY STUBBINS as they walk to DR. DOOLITTLE'S HOUSE. A long line of dogs follows them.]

TOMMY: How did he get to know so much about animals?

[MATTHEW stops his cart and leans over to whisper in TOMMY'S ear.]

MATTHEW: HE TALKS THEIR LANGUAGE.

POEM

How did he come to know so much
About cows and dogs and birds and such?

The cat's-meat-man whispered in my ear,
Words that no one else could hear:

"He talks their language. He speaks their way.
He listens to what they have to say."

PROSE

"How did he get to know so much about animals?" I asked.

The cat's-meat-man stopped and leant down to whisper in my ear.

"HE TALKS THEIR LANGUAGE," he said in a hoarse, mysterious voice.

by Hugh Lofting

To tell a story in prose, we use sentences. To tell a story with a poem we use short phrases or groups of words.

When a story is performed as a play, it is called a drama. Can you see the stage directions? They let the actors know when and where things happen.

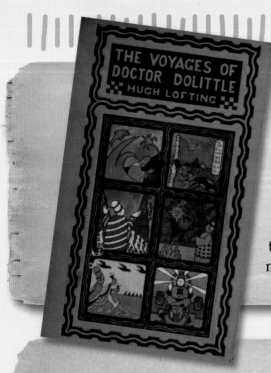

The Voyages of Dr. Doolittle

The Voyages of Dr. Doolittle was written by Hugh Lofting. It won the Newbery medal in 1923. In this story, Tommy Stubbins meets Dr. Doolittle. Tommy wants to become his assistant. The doctor is trying to find Long Arrow. Long Arrow was not easy to find. He traveled all over the world to study nature. He was the greatest **naturalist** in the world. Tommy and the doctor travel together to find him. Along the way, they visit many new lands. They even go under the sea.

Chapter 2

"How did he get to know so much about animals?" I asked.

The cat's-meat-man stopped and leant down to whisper in my ear.

"HE TALKS THEIR LANGUAGE," he said in a hoarse, mysterious voice.

"The animals' language?" I cried.

"Why certainly," said Matthew. "All animals have some kind of a language. Some sorts talk more than others; some only speak in sign-language, like deaf-and-dumb. But the Doctor, he understands them all—birds as well as animals. We keep it a secret though, him and me, because folks only laugh at you when you speak of it. Why, he can even write animal-language. He reads aloud to his pets. He's wrote history-books in monkey-talk, poetry in canary language and comic songs for magpies to sing. It's a fact. He's now busy learning the language of the shellfish. But he says it's hard work—and he has caught some terrible colds, holding his head under water so much. He's a great man."

"He certainly must be," I said. "I do wish he were home so I could meet him."

"Well, there's his house, look," said the cat's-meat-man—"that little one at the bend in the road there—the one high up—like it was sitting on the wall above the street."

We were now come beyond the edge of the town. And the house that Matthew pointed out was quite a small one standing by itself. There seemed to be a big garden around it; and this garden was much higher than the road, so you had to go up a flight of steps in the wall before you reached the front gate at the top. I could see that there were many fine fruit trees in the garden, for their branches hung down over the wall in places. But the wall was so high I could not see anything else.

When we reached the house Matthew went up the steps to the front gate and I followed him. I thought he was going to go into the garden; but the gate was locked. A dog came running down from the house; and he took several pieces of meat which the cat's-meat-man pushed through the bars of the gate, and some paper bags full of corn and bran, I noticed that this dog did not stop to eat the meat, as any ordinary dog would have done, but he took all the things back to the house and disappeared. He had a curious wide collar round his neck which looked as though it were made of brass or something. Then we came away.

"The Doctor isn't back yet," said Matthew, "or the gate wouldn't be locked."

"What were all those things in paper-bags you gave the dog?" I asked.

"Oh, those were provisions," said Matthew—"things for the animals to eat. The Doctor's house is simply full of pets. I give the things to the dog, while the Doctor's away, and the dog gives them to the other animals."

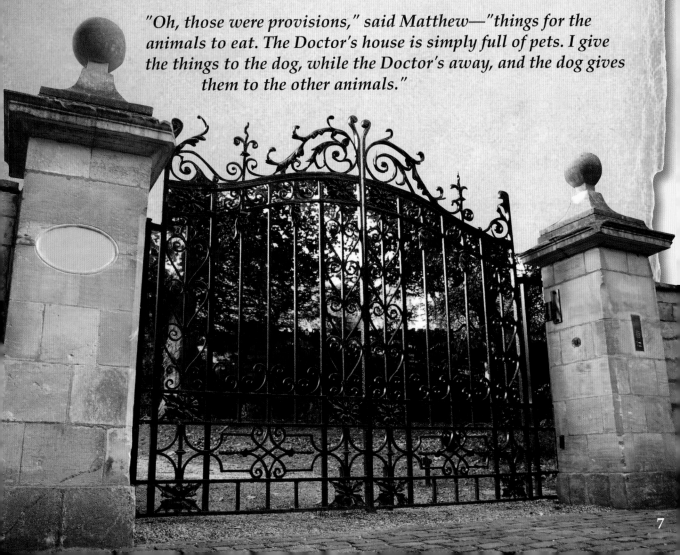

"And what was that curious collar he was wearing round his neck?"

"That's a solid gold dog-collar," said Matthew. "It was given to him when he was with the Doctor on one of his voyages long ago. He saved a man's life."

"How long has the Doctor had him?" I asked.

"Oh, a long time. Jip's getting pretty old now. That's why the Doctor doesn't take him on his voyages any more. He leaves him behind to take care of the house. Every Monday and Thursday I bring the food to the gate here and give it him through the bars. He never lets any one come inside the garden while the Doctor's away—not even me, though he knows me well. But you'll always be able to tell if the Doctor's back or not—because if he is, the gate will surely be open."

So I went off home to my father's house and put my squirrel to bed in an old wooden box full of straw. And there I nursed him myself and took care of him as best I could till the time should come when the Doctor would return. And every day I went to the little house with the big garden on the edge of the town and tried the gate to see if it were locked. Sometimes the dog, Jip, would come down to the gate to meet me. But though he always wagged his tail and seemed glad to see me, he never let me come inside the garden.

CHARACTERS IN ADVENTURE STORIES

The way a character acts is called a trait. They can be curious and ask a lot of questions. They can be impatient and not like to wait. Sometimes they are disobedient. **These traits can lead the character into an adventure.**

Characters in adventure stories face danger and excitement. Sometimes the main character is brave and daring. Other times, the main character is timid and afraid. They are forced to face their fears.

What clues do we have about Tommy's character?

Things the character says	character traits
"I do wish he were home so I could meet him."	Tommy is friendly.
"But the wall was so high I could not see anything else"	He is a small boy.
"What were all those things in paper-bags you gave the dog?"	He is curious, and asks a lot of questions.
"And what was that curious collar he was wearing round his neck?"	

Now continue the chart for the characters Matthew and Dr. Doolittle. Find examples in the text of things they say or do. Or look for things others say about them. This will show you their character traits.

SHOW DON'T TELL

As characters face and overcome **obstacles**, they change. Sometimes they may become more mature. They might be more sure of themselves. Other times, they might become more careful.

 Think of ways that Tommy might change after getting to know Dr. Doolittle. How could you show this in a story?

Make a new chart. This time, reverse the two columns. Imagine a trait Tommy might have at the end of the story. Write it in the column on the left. Now think of things he could say or do to show this new trait.

Character traits	Things the character says or does
Example:	
Tommy cares about others.	Tommy tries to get the Doctor to take a vacation when he sees him working too hard.

DIALOGUE: FORMAL AND INFORMAL SPEECH

When characters speak to each other in a story, it is called dialogue. **You can tell it is dialogue because the words have quotation marks around them.**

The way characters speak can tell us a lot about them. Think about how people talk in real life. Kings speak very differently than farmers. Ordinary people use **informal** speech. Informal speech has pauses and filler words. Some of these are "well," "see," and "you know." People who are speaking informally also shorten words. These words are called **contractions**.

Look at Matthew's dialogue in the text:

"Well, there's his house, look," said the cat's-meat-man—"that little one at the bend in the road there—the one high up—like it was sitting on the wall above the street.""

He uses informal speech. Let's see how this would sound in formal speech:

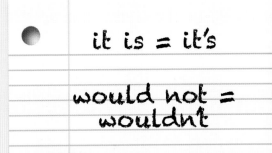

it is = it's

would not = wouldnt

"There is his house," said the cat's-meat-man, "It is that little one at the bend in the road. It sits high up. It looks like it was sitting on the wall above the street."

Think how the formal speech changes our idea of Matthew's character.

Formal speech has complete sentences with no filler words or contractions.

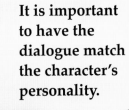

It is important to have the dialogue match the character's personality.

Dialogue has quotation marks around it. It also ends with a comma before the tag (he said/she said). For example, "I want to go home," said Janice.

SETTING: WHERE ARE WE?

> The setting is the time and location where a story takes place. It is sometimes called the story world. The setting helps us to "see" the story.

Adventure stories are often set in **exotic** places. Rudyard Kipling's *The Jungle Book* is set in the jungles of India. Sometimes they even take place in magical worlds. Wonderland in *Alice in Wonderland* is the strange world down the rabbit hole.

The Voyages of Dr. Doolittle begins in England. We can learn a lot about the setting by looking at the details in the story. We read that the Doctor's house was "beyond the edge of town." There "seemed to be a big garden around it." To see it "you had to go up a flight of steps in the wall before you reached the front gate at the top." Tommy couldn't see much of the garden because "the wall was so high."

England

> The author doesn't let us see all of the garden or house in this description. The high wall and the locked gate keep a sense of mystery about where the Doctor lives. This is a great place to start an adventure.

PLOT: A STORY IN THREE ACTS

The main events of a story are called the plot. Adventures stories are full of fast-paced action. The plot of an adventure story has three acts. They are the motivation, journey, and goal.

ACT II: THE JOURNEY

The journey is the trip the character takes. It is the main part of an adventure book. These are the steps our main character takes to reach their goal. This is where they will face all the dangers and obstacles in the story. Tommy, the Doctor, and all the animals find **stowaways** on board their ship. They also meet angry islanders and are in a shipwreck. Without a ship, they need to find a way back to England.

ACT I: MOTIVATION

The motivation starts the story moving. It is the reason the main character sets out on the adventure. Sometimes it comes from inside the main character. They might be a treasure hunter. Or they may be on a trip to explore the caves of Mexico. Sometimes the motivation comes from outside. It might be out of their control. They might have been kidnapped or stranded on a desert island. Tommy Stubbins' motivation is that he wants to study with Dr. Doolittle. He wants to become a naturalist.

ACT III: THE GOAL

The goal is the reward at the end of the story. The main character has survived. Maybe they have found the treasure or escaped from their kidnappers. In *The Voyages of Dr. Doolittle*, Tommy is relieved. The Doctor finally learns to speak to shellfish. He asks the giant sea snail to take them all back to England.

THEME: WHAT IS IT ABOUT?

The main idea of a story is called the theme. **The theme is woven through the story. Many adventure stories have themes of good and evil. Other themes are survival, facing your fears, and man and nature.**

In *The Voyages of Dr. Doolittle*, we can see several themes. They are: **compassion**, understanding, and concern for all living things.

Compassion

Dr. Doolittle goes to court to help defend Bob the dog on his murder charge.

Understanding

Polynesia the parrot helps Tommy learn to speak to the animals.

Concern

Dr. Doolittle becomes the new king of the Popsipetels. He works hard to improve the lives of the tribe.

The moral is the lesson the author wants us to take away from the story. These morals are often about never giving up in difficult situations. They are also about facing your fears. Think about the challenges Tommy faced on his journey.

- How did he change?

- What do you think the moral themes of this story might be?

 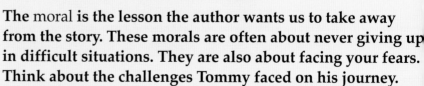

Jip the dog decides to let you in the garden. He unlocks the gate. Describe what the Doctor's walled garden looks like. What animals might be in there?

The Doctor speaks several different animal languages. Pick an animal and create a dialogue between the animal and Dr. Doolittle. Have the animal talk to him about going along on his next trip. Remember to make their speech match their personality.

Imagine your pet, or a neighbor's pet, could talk. How would he or she describe you? What name would he or she give you?

BLACK BEAUTY

The main characters in an adventure story are not always people. Animals can have adventures, too. Dogs, cats, horses, birds, and dolphins are just some of the animals that are in these stories.

Buck is the heroic **dog in the novel** *The Call of the Wild.* **He was stolen from his home. Then he was sold as a sled dog during the Gold Rush in Alaska.**

Black Beauty is the story of a horse living in England. He lived at a time before cars. Back then, people traveled with horse and buggy. Beauty made and lost friends. He also had many adventures. He was ridden, driven, and he pulled a cab in London.

Chapter 16 The Fire

Later on in the evening a traveler's horse was brought in by the second hostler, and while he was cleaning him a young man with a pipe in his mouth lounged into the stable to gossip.

"I say, Towler," said the hostler, "just run up the ladder into the loft and put some hay down into this horse's rack, will you? only lay down your pipe."

"All right," said the other, and went up through the trapdoor; and I heard him step across the floor overhead and put down the hay. James came in to look at us the last thing, and then the door was locked.

I cannot say how long I had slept, nor what time in the night it was, but I woke up very uncomfortable, though I hardly knew why. I got up; the air seemed all thick and choking. I heard Ginger coughing and one of the other horses seemed very restless; it was quite dark, and I could see nothing, but the stable seemed full of smoke, and I hardly knew how to breathe.

The trapdoor had been left open, and I thought that was the place it came through. I listened, and heard a soft rushing sort of noise and a low crackling and snapping. I did not know what it was, but there was something in the sound so strange that it made me tremble all over. The other horses were all awake; some were pulling at their halters, others stamping.

At last I heard steps outside, and the hostler who had put up the traveler's horse burst into the stable with a lantern, and began to untie the horses, and try to lead them out; but he seemed in such a hurry and so frightened himself that he frightened me still more. The first horse would not go with him; he tried the second and third, and they too would not stir. He came to me next and tried to drag me out of the stall by force; of course that was no use. He tried us all by turns and then left the stable.

No doubt we were very foolish, but danger seemed to be all round, and there was nobody we knew to trust in, and all was strange and uncertain. The fresh air that had come in through the open door made it easier to breathe, but the rushing sound overhead grew louder, and as I looked upward through the bars of my empty rack I saw a red light flickering on the wall. Then I heard a cry of "Fire!" outside, and the old hostler quietly and quickly came in; he got one horse out, and went to another, but the flames were playing round the trapdoor, and the roaring overhead was dreadful.

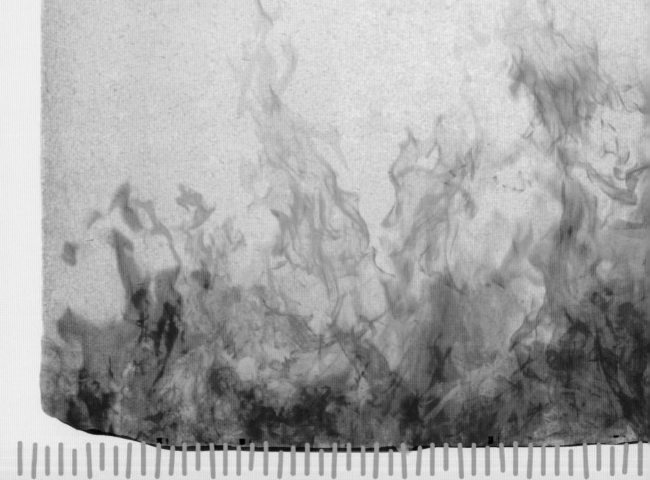

The next thing I heard was James' voice, quiet and cheery, as it always was.

"Come, my beauties, it is time for us to be off, so wake up and come along." I stood nearest the door, so he came to me first, patting me as he came in.

"Come, Beauty, on with your bridle, my boy, we'll soon be out of this smother." It was on in no time; then he took the scarf off his neck, and tied it lightly over my eyes, and patting and coaxing he led me out of the stable. Safe in the yard, he slipped the scarf off my eyes, and shouted, "Here somebody! Take this horse while I go back for the other."

A tall, broad man stepped forward and took me, and James darted back into the stable. I set up a shrill whinny as I saw him go. Ginger told me afterward that whinny was the best thing I could have done for her, for had she not heard me outside she would never have had courage to come out.

When we experience the world around us, we don't just use our eyes. We hear things, we smell things, and we touch things. When an author describes the setting in a story, all five senses should be used. This helps the reader really understand where and when the story is taking place.

There are lots of ways to describe people, places, or things with our senses:

Sense	Descriptive Words
Sight	Bright, gloomy, towering, colorful
Smell	Musty, smoky, flowery
Hearing	Rustling, chirping, gurgling
Taste	Salty, sweet, crunchy, bitter
Touch	Rough, smooth, knotted, wet

Can you think of more descriptive words for each sense?

In *Black Beauty,* the author describes smells, sounds, touch as well as sight. This helps the reader imagine what the fire was like for the horses trapped in the barn.

Sounds
- soft rushing
- low crackling
- snapping, shrill whinny

Sights
- red light flickering
- flames were playing round the trapdoor

Smells
- the air seemed all thick and choking
- full of smoke

Touch
- patting me
- tied it lightly over my eyes

It is important to use as many different senses as you can when describing something. This will make help readers really feel like they are inside the story.

POINT OF VIEW: WHO IS TALKING?

A story can be told in different ways.

Sometimes it is told as if the reader was seeing the events through the eyes of the main character. This is called first person **point of view**. The author uses the words "I" or "we":

 "The first place that I can well remember was a large pleasant meadow with a pond of clear water in it." *Black Beauty*

Sometimes it is told as though the author were talking directly to the reader. This is called second person point of view. The author uses the pronoun "you":

 "If you could keep awake (but of course you can't) you would see your own mother doing this, and you would find it very interesting to watch her." *Peter Pan*

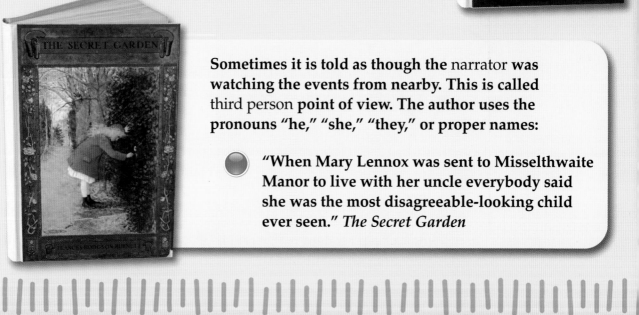

Sometimes it is told as though the narrator was watching the events from nearby. This is called third person **point of view**. The author uses the pronouns "he," "she," "they," or proper names:

 "When Mary Lennox was sent to Misselthwaite Manor to live with her uncle everybody said she was the most disagreeable-looking child ever seen." *The Secret Garden*

A FIRST-PERSON ADVENTURE

Black Beauty is told in first person. We see what is happening through Beauty's eyes. We get to imagine what it is like to be a horse living at that time.

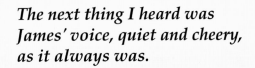

> *The next thing I heard was James' voice, quiet and cheery, as it always was.*
>
> *"Come, my beauties, it is time for us to be off, so wake up and come along." I stood nearest the door, so he came to me first, patting me as he came in.*

COMPARE AND CONTRAST

The Voyages of Dr. Doolittle and *Black Beauty* are both adventure stories. They are both told in the first person point of view. But not everything in these two stories is alike. Think about their settings, dialogue, and themes. How are they similar? How are they different? Select two items from these two adventure stories that interest you. Make a chart to compare them. Then write a compare-and-contrast essay.

PLOT: A MAP OF THE STORY

The plot is the roadmap of the story.
All stories follow a basic pattern:

PLOT MAP
A plot map can help you outline your adventure story.

Climax

Resolution

Rising
Action

Inciting
Incident

Introduction

Introduction: We get to know the characters and the setting.

Inciting Incident: An event that starts the character on their journey.

Rising Action: Problems and obstacles in the character's way.

Climax: The main character faces their problem.

Resolution: Events are wrapped up in a satisfying way.

In *Black Beauty* we can see this same pattern:

Introduction: We meet Black Beauty, Duchess, and their owner.

Inciting Incident: Black Beauty is sold and begins his life as a working horse.

Rising Action: Beauty works at several different jobs for both kind and cruel owners.

Climax: Beauty is badly injured and may lose his life.

Resolution: An old man and his grandson rescue Beauty. Beauty lives out his life with a kind family.

THEME: WHAT IS IT ABOUT?

Many adventure stories are about finding your way home. These stories often take place on deserted islands or deep in jungles. Sometimes the journey home is not about exotic places. It might be about finding the place where you belong.

In this story, Black Beauty's last home is with three kind ladies at Rose Hall. Their groom is Joe Green. He was the young groom who used to look after Black Beauty where he was born. Explain how Black Beauty fits the theme of "finding your way home."

The author wants the reader to learn some important lessons about the value of kindness. Beauty goes through difficult times with cruel owners. Even so, he never turns mean or bitter. The author also shows that Beauty's kindness is rewarded when he finds a good home in the end.

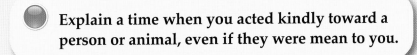

Explain a time when you acted kindly toward a person or animal, even if they were mean to you.

CREATIVE RESPONSE TO THE ADVENTURE STORY

Write the opening of *Black Beauty* from another point of view. How would the story sound from Black Beauty's mother, the master, or Dick?

Think of the words that can create different moods for a story. Describe a park or playground near your home. Give the setting a mood with your description.

In the story *Black Beauty*, horses have many uses. They are used for transportation and farming. Today, horses are used for many other things. They are ridden on trail rides and rodeos. They perform in horse shows and at fairs. They are used for horse-and-carriage rides. Police ride horses, too. If you were a horse or pony today, what would your ideal job be?

WRITING AN ADVENTURE STORY

1. PREWRITING

Choose an Adventure

Think of the type of adventure story you want to write. Will it be:

- treasure hunt
- dangerous mission
- **expedition** to a strange land
- survival story
- journey home

Sample:

Type of Adventure Story: Treasure hunt for lost **legendary** sword.

2. What a Character!

Who will your main character be? Will this person be brave and daring, and will they go looking for adventure? Or will your character be timid? Will events force him or her to do something amazing? Does this person have a big fear or a great love?

Sample:

Main Character: Molly Spencer, daughter of archaeologist

Traits: Hates history, wants to spend summer at water park, has to go with her mother on a dig.

Where and When?

Imagine the setting of your story. An adventure can happen anywhere. Big cities can be as wild and dangerous as a jungle. Will your story start in an ordinary place? Then will it move to an exotic location? Think of the time in history, too. Will your story take place long ago or in the present day?

Sample:

Setting: Story opens in North America. Characters fly to England. Dig site is in the shadow of castle ruins. It is modern times and a cold, damp summer.

Three Acts

Think about the motivation, journey, and goal of your main character. What makes your main character begin their adventure? Does he or she:

- find a clue to a treasure or amazing item
- learn about a mysterious place they want to explore
- become lost because of a storm, accident, or kidnapper

What obstacles and problems will your character have to overcome? Will they have to face their biggest fear?

What is their goal? Make it something big and important. Often adventure stories are a matter of life and death. What will your character lose if they do not reach this goal? What will they learn from achieving their goal?

Sample:

Motivation: Has to spend summer with mother at dig site or be stuck with relatives babysitting younger cousins.

Journey: Discoveries at the site
Finding a hidden tunnel under the ruins
Someone is sabotaging the site

Goal: Molly wants to find the legendary sword.

Write Your First Draft

Write down your story. Look at your notes about your character's motivation that will send him or her on his way. Remember to put lots of obstacles and problems in his or her way. Include lots of fast-paced action. Keep that goal in sight.

Sample:

Find something useful to do, Molly's mother told her. Molly kicked at the pile of dirt. I wish I was doing something else she said to no one in particular. She wandered away from all the others. Suddenly the ground collapsed under her feet. She had fallen into a large cave. Molly saw something. It was a sword! She picked it up and it began to hum.

Revise Your Story

Many authors say that a story comes to life in the revision. This is a good time to take a look at what you have written and make improvements.

● Can you point out the introduction, inciting incident, rising action, climax, and resolution of your story?

● Does your dialogue match the personality and age of your characters?

● Do you use all five senses when describing people, places, and things in your story?

● Have you created tension by challenging your main character?

Sample:

Find something useful to do, Molly's mother told her.

Molly kicked at the pile of dirt. It was so hard it hurt her toe.

Working at a dig site is boring she said to no one in particular.

She wandered away from all the others. The ground hear looked different. It was loose and grey. Suddenly the ground collapsed under her feet. She had fallen into a large cave. It was musty and damp inside. Molly saw something glittering at the back. It was a sword! She struggled to pick it up; it was so heavy. When she did, it began to hum.

Proofread Your Adventure Story

Proofreading means checking for spelling, grammar, and punctuation.

- Check for words that sound the same but are spelled differently, such as: their, they're, and there. Are they used properly?
- Double check that your dialogue has the correct punctuation.
- Make sure all proper names of people and places are capitalized.

Some authors find it helpful to read a story out loud to catch mistakes.

Sample

"Find something useful to do," Molly's mother told her.

Molly kicked at the pile of dirt. It was so hard it hurt her toe.

"Working at a dig site is boring," she said to no one in particular.

She wandered away from all the others. The ground here looked different. It was loose and grey. Suddenly the ground collapsed beneath her feet. She had fallen into a large cave. It was musty and damp inside.

Molly saw something glittering at the back. It was a sword! She struggled to pick it up; it was so heavy. When she did, it began to hum.

Final Copy

Now it is time to rewrite or retype a clean, neat, error-free copy of your story.

GLOSSARY

Please note: Some bold-faced words are defined in the text

compassion	Concern for the suffering of other people
disobedient	Refusing to obey the rules
exotic	Unusual or strange and coming from far away
expedition	A trip taken for scientific research or discovery
gurgling	Hollow bubbling sound
heroic	Very brave
inciting	To stir something to action
informal	A relaxed, friendly style
legendary	Famous or well known from long ago
narrator	The person telling the story
naturalist	A person who studies nature
obstacles	Something that blocks the way
stowaways	People or animals hiding onboard a ship

INDEX

Alice's Adventures in Wonderland 12
Black Beauty 16–26
character traits 9, 10, 27
characters 9–10, 27
compare and contrast 23
creative responses 15, 26
dialogue 11, 15, 23, 29, 30
drafts 29, 30
dramas 5
facing fears 9, 14, 27, 28
goals 13, 28

journeys 13, 14, 24, 25, 27, 28
Jungle Book, The 12
Kidnapped 4
morals 14
motivation 13, 28
obstacles 10, 13, 24, 28, 29
plots 13, 24
poems 5
point of view 22–23
proofreading 30
prose 5

revisions 29
senses 20–21, 29
settings 12, 20, 23, 24, 26, 28
Swiss Family Robinson 4
themes 14, 23, 25
types of adventures 4, 27
Voyages of Dr. Doolittle, The 5–15
writing an adventure 27–30

FURTHER RESOURCES

Books:

Adventure Stories (Writing Stories) by Anita Ganeri. Raintree (2013)

Adventure Stories (It's Fun To Write) by Ruth Thomson. Sea to Sea Publications (2012)

Illustrated Adventure Stories by Lesley Sims. Usborne Books (2011)

The Voyages of Dr. Doolittle (Classic Starts) by Hugh Lofting. Sterling (2008)

Black Beauty by Anna Sewell. Signet Classics (2011)

Websites:
Adventure stories online :
www.bedtimestoriesonline.org/adventure-stories/

This site lists all kinds of adventure books for kids according to type:
http://kidsadventurebooks.com